HIS PhD IS IN HYPOCRISY

...AND OTHER POEMS ABOUT MY CRAPPY EX-BOYFRIEND

TAYO OREDEIN

LCCN: 20149335997
ISBN: 978-0-6159-8321-9

Gynarchy
PO Box 120354
Saint Albans, NY 11412

Cover Design by Tayo Oredein
Front Cover Photo © 2000 Tayo Oredein
Author Photo © 2013 Sean Bernard

Acknowledgments

I thank my God for giving me breath, my family for giving me love, my friends for giving me strength, and my ex for giving me angst. Without even one of these components, I would not have been able to write these words.

Thanks for checking out this book. It would be amazing if you reviewed it on Amazon, Goodreads, FB, etc... and dont forget to pass it along to the next wellesley sib

xoxo

tayo '98

Author's Note

In 2000, I fell in love for the first time and then I had my heart crushed.

This series of poems began with my need to get past the hurt, and to heal. As time went on, it spawned into a literary project of sorts. As I chronicled the relationship through poetry, I began to see that everything, even heartache, happens for a reason.

HIS PhD IS IN HYPOCRISY

...AND OTHER POEMS ABOUT MY CRAPPY EX-BOYFRIEND

Table of Poetry

Our Beginning

A Love Like This

Our Beginning

First Date   *October 2, '99*
A nervous me ironed out my clothes-
Black jeans and a white shirt.
A nervous me pulled my hair back-
I'd wear it in a low bun.
A nervous me polished my nails-
No flaws allowed.
A nervous me painted my lips-
Bronzed, red kissed by the sun.

A nervous me peeked out the window
but no one was there yet.
So a nervous me chatted with my folks
as I waited for my date to arrive
A nervous me jumped up
when the bell finally rang
My date was at the front door
It was seven twenty-five

He was still as cute as ever
with his eyes blazing blue
He wore blue jeans, a green shirt
a funky hat, and a tan vest
I admired his appearance
His healthy beard nicely trimmed
He was nice, clean and neat
I liked the way he was dressed

1

A nervous me sat next to him
during dinner at Pizzeria Uno's
I enjoyed our conversation and my food
for which, he wouldn't let me pay
We went to shoot pool afterwards
where he proceeded to sing
"Back That Ass Up" by Juvenile
whenever I bent over to play

Our last stop before my house was the bay
out on the rocks, out in the water
Looking up, he named nearby stars
in an opportunity too good to miss,
when he looked back down
a nervous, but now gutsy me
pulled him in for a deep kiss

The First Two Months   _November '99_
In the first two months, there were four dates
Each time we went out
I had a lot of fun with him
but, soon I begin to have doubts

We were supposed to double date once
with my best friend and her man
He called to cancel at the last minute
but was surprised when I went through with my plans

That wasn't the first time,
It sure as hell wasn't the last
Often times he'd cancel after
our meeting time had passed

Phone calls from him were rare,
unless making plans for later that night
Usually we'd end up seeing a movie
maybe to grab a bite

A week or more would pass
without so much as a phone call
What the hell is up with this guy?
Doesn't he like me at all?

I really thought he didn't
It sure as hell seemed that way
I hardly saw or heard from him;
At best every other Sunday

Is there another girl
that he is seeing?
Is there someone else
With whom he liked being?

With curiosity running the show
I had to know if I was the only one
So I asked if there were other girls
He told me there were none

In unrelated events, the next Friday
I was going to Boston to see
Some friends from college.
He said he'd accompany me

Then he said he wasn't sure
He'd let me know soon
Finally, he told me he couldn't go
That was Thursday afternoon

He said Ramadan was the reason
Saying one shouldn't fast when he travels
So there was a conflict of interest
He didn't want his religious fiber to unravel

Whatever! I'd go by myself
I had no problem with it
I was just sad because then I *knew*
there was no chance for a relationship

Two months had passed
since we had our first kiss
And look what happened
I had indisputably been dissed

My Trip to Boston   *December 10, '99*
I wish he had come up
I just know we would have had fun
But I gotta face reality
Our time- It's done
He hardly ever calls
and rarely tries to see me
There's nothing that even says
he wants to be with me

So while I'm up here
I'm not going to think about it
I'm just going to chill with friends
Drink 'til I forget
There are some cuties here
Some looking my way
Oh, but not Sean
No, that guy's gay

But this guy here,
Hmm, he's kind of cute
Oh, you picked up on my joke
My, how astute
What's that you went to BU?
Oh my best friend went there
Maybe you've seen her-
Pretty, Puerto-Rican-Peruvian,
With really long hair

Why yes I'd love to dance,
No thanks I already have a drink
Yea, I love this song too
They just took a picture of us I think
This is a cool party
Interesting people all around
There's good food, and drink
And good music with surround sound

Wow, what a night
It ended kind of late
Kick back and watch a movie?
Sure, sounds great
Let me sit on the couch
and watch the screen
I don't think this movie
is one I'd ever seen
Yes, I'm quite comfortable
Thank you very much
Wait a minute now
How did our lips touch?
The kiss was quick
Only three seconds had passed
But my mind was on that stupid New York guy
So I pulled away fast

Why can't I get this guy
out of my bloody head
He doesn't even like me
Our relationship is dead
Still I keep thinking of him
Even with this cute guy here
I only want Steven
I see that now, it's clear

My Cell   *December 13, '99*

My cell's been ringing
with calls from my mother,
calls from my friends,
and calls from some others
Imagine my surprise
when my phone rang
and his number showed up
on the caller ID
Oh my gosh!
He called me
Mostly to say hi,
But also to say
he's going to meet me
at the bus station
when I come home Sunday
Wow, maybe just maybe
there *are* feelings on his end too
I can't wait to get back to NY
so I can become his boo

What Fast?   *December 14, '99*

I'm back home in New York
And things haven't changed
I hardly hear from the boy
No new dates have been arranged

And what's this- he goes to DC this weekend?
Apparently unconcerned with breaking his fast
So why couldn't he go to Boston with me?
Humph Ramadan, my ASS!!!

Why?   *December 15, '99*

Why do I pursue him?
Why do I like him so much?
He's funny, that's true
and gorgeous indeed,
with nice, full lips
and eyes so blue

But there's more to it than that
I like spending time with him
He has a lot to say
He's very intelligent
and we engage in real discussions-
I could talk with him all day

That's a lot right there
But you could add to that
I like his style
the clothes he wears,
the way he wears them,
his beautiful smile

7

To have him in my life
To hold him in my arms...
would bring such pleasure
joy and delight,
ecstasy and mirth,
Wonderful feelings beyond measure

Butterflies   *December 16, '99*

I can't stand up straight
Crippled with butterflies
They're flying around inside
reminding me of my infatuation

They don't leave me alone
They pain me morning, noon and night
Heaven forbid I should speak his name
I'm dead if I hear his voice

They're so intense
and very relentless
This boy's all up in my system
If only I can get him all up in my life

Confused   *December 18, '99*

Does he like me, or no?
So many signals
Confuse me so
I don't know which way
Is up, left, right,
Or which way to go

We see each other every other week
Maybe a movie, pool, chilling at his house
or grabbing a bite to eat
But it doesn't get much deeper than that
which makes me think
That my chances are pretty bleak

He likes me he confessed,
though I know that doesn't necessarily mean
that I'm his love interest
I make it a point to look nice when I see him
to try to look my best
But I still don't think he's all that impressed

"Relationships," the ranting began
"Are backwards in theory
Because its participants demand
the benefits of marriage
But they have no real claims
since there's no wedding band"

Ok, now I'm really befuddled
Was this a hint?
Was he trying to be subtle?
He had a valid point
about the whole girlfriend-boyfriend thing
But, ok, here is my rebuttal

Given all that, he was still cool
to give three years to his college girlfriend
and two to the one he had in high school
So relationships with him
Were not out of the question
So why couldn't he give me one too?

I could sit around holding my hand
being unsure of myself and of us
or I can take a stand.
The next time I see him
I'm going to take a deep breath
And ask him to be my man

December 19, 1999   *December 19, 1999*
He has reservations
about being my man
But I'll ask him just the same
and if he wants to decline
Well, then he can

He just came back from DC
and called me for a date
And I asked him that day
to be my mate

To my surprise, he said yes
He'd be my man
I never would have guessed

There was no more need for me to pretend
As of December 19, 1999 I was his girlfriend

Then vs. Now

December 31, '99

On December 19, I became his girl whereas
he dates us back to October second-
the day of our first date
Funny how though,
it was only after the 19th of December
that I can remember
seeing him more often,
going out with friends,
both his and mine-
to dinners, shows, movies, and parties,
and chilling in his house.
Steady phone calls,
talking more,
more intimate chats.
Ringing in the New Year together.
Year 2000-the big one at that
I'm not complaining about the difference
Just making an observation
Unless the way things were
those first two months
was only my imagination

A Love Like This

He Loves Me   *January '00*
We're standing in my basement
Just come in from a wonderful date
Kissing each other good-bye
"I love your lips" I tell him....

"I love *you*"
"You say that like you mean it"
 "I do"

Family Smiles   *January '00*
I sit with his father in the kitchen
An animated, witty man,
He talks about Islam
and other things important to him
I am listening intently
He's smiling at me when he talks
A charming smile
A sincere smile
I think he likes me

Steve sits beside me
listening to the dialogue
jumping in whenever to
contribute his piece

Smiling at his father and me
A smile like his father's,
Sincere and charming
I know he likes me

His mother comes in next
Hugs me tightly,
and invites me for dinner
I graciously accept
She smiles at me too
A delightful smile
A sincere smile
I think she likes me

His brother comes home
and hugs me too
He chats with me a little
before we all sit to eat
His smile too is charming
and sincere
when he talks to me
Such a nice family
I know I like them

Interracial Troubles   **_January '00_**
Interracial that's for sure
I wonder if our relationship can endure
the tests that will be put forth
I know I like you,
race and skin color aside
but I wonder why you're with me-
because I'm black?
An experience you've never had?
Or do you think dating black is "cool"

13

If that's the case I want out
I'm not your guinea pig
But what's this?
You want to be with me for me?
And you're interested in my history?
You can appreciate black culture,
without trying to adopt it as your own?
You don't belittle my concerns and
instead encourage me to talk about them?
I guess I underestimated you,
I underestimated us
I'm glad I found someone I can talk to
Someone who will listen to me
Someone I can trust

Fallin' Hard, Fallin' Fast   February '00
Sleeping in his arms
Waking up to his lips
How I love this man
Wait, did I say "love"?
I did say love, didn't I?
I meant it too
I can't believe how hard I fell
Or how fast either
How can this be?
We've only been together
a short while
So how is it then that I know
I want to be his wife-
of course in the years to come.
How did it come to be
I only want to be with him?
that no other man turns my head?
Someone please tell me

what spell has been cast
To make me fall this hard
and this fast?

Never a Kiss   *February '00*

Never a kiss so sweet
Never one so tender
Never a kiss so intimate
Never a kiss to make me so wet
The softness of your mouth
Your tongue tracing my lips
Your fingers running through my hair
Things getting damp down there
Cradling your face
and you cradling mine
Never a kiss so full of bliss
Never a kiss so perfect as this

The Ex at the Club   *February '00*

Asian, short, petite, cute face, long hair
Dark, blue denim skirt clinging to her hips
as she dances beside me
singing through pursed lips
I didn't know who she was at the time,
but I knew she was an ex of some kind
Women's intuition is a powerful thing.
Later I'd find out she was in fact his ex
His ex-girlfriend, to be specific
The one to whom he gave three years-
Though not all those years were hers alone
She was sharing him with other girls
unbeknownst to her for some while

When the truth came to her,
To use his word, she "flipped"
But she still stayed
and for a stretch,
She was the only one to experience him
But once again, he strayed
He says because he was displeased with her
sighting questionable moves she made
earlier in the relationship
If she cheated too, I can't be sure
but they both had ways to hurt each other,
Ways to make the pain endure
Eventually it drove them apart
and there, they stayed
I don't know if she loved him
And when I asked if he loved her
He simply replied "I guess"...
So here I am, being introduced to this woman
and while she clearly feigned interest
She shook my hand and smiled gracefully
then disappeared into the crowd
As quickly as she could-
The same way I'm sure she wished
her ex and I would

My Arabic   *February '00*
His culture is important to him
Therefore it's important to me
So for him I'll try to learn
to speak in "Arabee"
So far I can read it and write it
I just can't understand
But I can say a few things
in the language of his land

We all know "As-asallam wa al-laikem"
and it's response "wa aleikem assalam"
Ok, now to say "no" you say "laa"
and for "yes", you say "naam"

"Marhaba" means "hello"
"Maasalaama" is "good-bye"
and "thank you" is "shukran"
to which "Afwan" is the reply

When you express a hope,
"If God wills it" is "In Shallah",
to say "hurry up",
you utter "Y'allah"

"How are you" is "Keif halac"
and you respond with the phrase
"Al humduillah", a kind of "thanks",
giving God His praise

So here I have my few words
just to get my foot in "al baab", the door
now I must go study, so for now
"Khallas", or in English "no more"

Islam   February '00

My family raised me to be a Christian
My baby was raised Muslim
So I read up a little on his religion
in order to better understand him

They believe in one God
as in Judaism and Christianity
But Muslims differ from Christians
in that we believe in the Trinity

Muslims believe it is just God, or Allah
with no Son or Holy Ghost
I don't know much about what Jews think
but Muslims and Jews seem to clash the most

They are both descendants of Abraham
The Jews are from his youngest Isaac
The Muslims are from Ishmeal,
Born to Hagar, believed to be black.

There are five pillars of Islam
The first of which is to declare
Allah as the only and supreme ruler
to whom nothing or no one can compare

And that Muhammad is His messenger
A descendent of Ishmael's line
who devoted his entire life serving Allah,
the most high and most divine

He served Allah wholeheartedly
gladly accepting when he was called upon
to bring God's message to earth
and live his life in the way of the Q'uran

The second pillar is prayer
which must be made five times a day
during the appropriate intervals
and in a particular way

One must rid the body of physical impurities
You must wash hands, arms, feet and hair too
and rinse your nostrils, and mouth thrice
This is the state of "wudu"

To touch a member of the opposite sex
who is not your father or mother, sister or brother
Means you have broken your wudu
and you must perform another

Then one makes prayer,
Kneeling towards the rising sun
Praising Allah's name
Reciting suras from the Q'uran

The third pillar is the Zakat
A tax to be given to the poor
It's due once every year
for those who have been blessed with more

The fourth is fasting
during the month of Ramadan
following the guidelines
dictated by the Q'uran

Here is the fifth and final
Every woman and man
must make a pilgrimage to Mecca
for worship and prayer in the holy land

There are other random bits
of Islamic knowledge I acquired
About daily customs, family life
and men and women's attire

"Bismilah irahman iraheem"
is what you say over a meal of halal meat,
Meaning the meat was killed in Allah's name
It's the only kind are they allowed to eat

Under no circumstances
is any kind of pork,
Regardless of the part,
allowed to touch their fork

And the men, they should have beards
and are praised for facial hair
Ironically enough, they're supposed to
pluck some other areas bare.

There are a lot of other rules
But they're not all that complex
In fact other religions go by them too:
No overindulgence, drugs or pre-marital sex

Though one thing other religions forbid
is tolerated in a Muslim's life
For example, if he so chooses,
a Muslim man may have more than one wife

And their men can marry a woman
if she's Muslim, Christian or a Jew
But their women can only have one husband,
and he has to be Muslim too

Muslim law goes on to say
the females should cover their hair
and in fact most parts of their body
which, for me, would be a nightmare

There's a lot more to the religion
including gender-oriented details
which to me seems to certainly favor
the men over the females

I admit there are parts of Islam
that make sense to me
But I am just a spectator for now
I'm not planning to leave my Christianity

Imagine That   ***February '00***
Dark chocolate, medium brown
High yellow, or Spanish gold
Wavy hair, or nappy
It really didn't matter
Five-foot-six or as tall as six-foot-five
Weight was never an issue either
any size could make me happy
Seemingly the only physical attribute
was for a Black or Latino hue
So imagine my surprise
when the man I fell in love with was you-
As fair as they come
with straight hair and blue eyes
Baby I know you worry but
please don't be insecure
I generally date only men
who are Hispanic and Black
but it's only you who I want now
Hmm, imagine that

Why I'm With You   *March '00*

You are the only one with whom I want to be
I mean that emotionally, and of course sexually
It's not that I feel obligated because you're my man
We're not married, and I know we both can
therefore do what or whomever we want
But it's nice to know that we love each other so much
we're not interested in anyone else's touch
It's great to know, no other guy and no other girl
can come in and upset our near-perfect world
You've told me so many times that you only want me
and you should know by now, I feel mutually
We're together out of love, and not 'cuz there's a need
and for that, I feel very privileged indeed
There's no one else I want or with whom I'd rather be
and I'm glad you feel the exact same way about me

True Confessions   *March '00*

It's night, and we're on the phone,
about two in the morning
Talking about our relationship
and he comes out with some news
Though he said he was only seeing me
during October and November
He was seeing another girl too
and didn't stop until mid-December
So that's why he didn't go with me to Boston
Hell, that's why he canceled on me so damn often
It was then I told him, about the guy that I kissed
that honestly it meant nothing to me,
and in fact, it had been completely dismissed
from my mind right after it happened
I hadn't thought about him again

Hell, I'd forgotten about him until then
Though Steve was ridiculously upset
Asking question after question
until I flipped it back on him
and out came another confession
When he went to DC,
The day before we became official
He met up and kissed Sandra
A girl who gave him her virginity
He was vague about what else happened that day
claiming it's not important now
Though he still asked about the guy
completely dismissing my inquiries about
why he felt the need to lie
So what does all this mean?
Where did the trust go, and
where do we go from here?
Is there a way this can be repaired?
That night we were on the phone
for a total of six hours
And the next day,
before we went out to dinner,
My darling brought a nervous, confused me
A beautiful bouquet of flowers

Different?   *March '00*

There's a pain in my heart
that grows stronger every day
because the man I'm in love with
has given so much of himself away
indiscriminately to such undeserving girls
And now there's very little left for me.
And how pure is whatever's left?
He says I'm special and different
but how can something be so special with me
when he's done the same thing with girls
too numerous to count
How can it be precious with me
when he's done the same thing with girls
regardless of how he felt
Almost any female met his requirements
There were not many disregarded factors
Women of all ages, races, creed, religion,
body type, and relations were accepted
As long as there was a functioning hole
between either set of lips, he was game
So how can it be different with me
when everything's so much the same?

A Rite of Passage   *March '00*

How could he share himself with so many?
His number rising exponentially
in college when he cheated on his ex
Using it as a scapegoat to deal with his feelings
and as a means to hurt her,
while pleasing himself for the moment
Perhaps there was more to his promiscuity
Maybe the notches in his belt
made up for an insecurity
by filling as many holes as he could,
somehow he was filling the one in his soul
How else could you engage in the physical act of love
with someone you hate so much
that you cringe when they speak?
That you book it out of there
the very moment after you peaked?
But maybe his intent there
was to hurt and humiliate,
To take something precious from them
and after, why not sleep with her roommate?
Being with him doesn't mean you're special
It doesn't mean he likes or cares for you either
It's not a privilege, more like a rite of passage
Making me wonder, are things really different with me
or is it just my turn to be his piece of ass

Pure   *March '00*

He's upset that I wasn't pure
when we got together
Haunted by the few men of my past
most of whom are mistakes
But who doesn't have those scars?
And why are *my* scars *his* open wounds?
No, he's not the first man in my life
but he equates that with ill intentions
And should I profess my love for him
he hears false words describing false emotions
He won't let himself see
how much I care, or how much he means to me
Doesn't he see the pain in my eyes
when he doubts my feelings?
Come to think of it,
doesn't he see the pain in my eyes
when the women he was with see me?
Smirking and laughing to themselves
knowing they've already had my man,
Turned him on and turned him out,
probably in a way I never could
Letting him push his love between their lips,
One set or another
And now, yes, he's with me
But not all of him is mine
Parts of him belong to them
And he holds on to pieces of his past concubines
So how can I be special
When I'm really just who's next,
Just another number.
Just another hole.
Just another conquest.
Just like them.
Just for sex.

You're Not Mine   **March '00**

You're not mine.
You're not mine!
I heard those words all the fucking time...
They ring in my ears
As you argue I belong to people before you
I tell you baby, that couldn't be more untrue
Just because you're not my first
doesn't mean I'm not your baby
Especially since I'd do almost anything
for you and for us
But see, I know you
I know you well
That's only part of your issue
Your ego makes you want to be my first,
even though I'm number twenty or thirty
Of course we can't say that with certainty-
That's just a ballpark figure
But even if you were my first,
there's no guarantee that things would be Ok
You'd find something else with which to push me away
Something else problematic
like you did with those whose first you were
Treating them poorly, and ignoring them
but making plenty of naked time
for their roommates and friends
It's Ok for you to have slept with all those chicks
with no rhyme or reason, save your horny mode
and should we split, you'd start all over again
probably just two days after we end
So by your definition, you can't be mine either.
Funny you're so upset with me
saying "You're not mine. You're not mine."
I still love you very much.
But I gotta tell you,
This shit is straight up asinine

My Friends Are Just That   *March 20, '00*

What exactly is your problem with my friends?
My friends are just that, my friends
I haven't slept with any them,
Male or female.
Yet you have issues beyond belief
Concerned that we've seen each other naked-
Or that at some point we're going to.
Why can't you get it through your thick bearded head
that my friends and I have never been to bed
Why don't you worry about you and your female friends
instead?

Problem number two?
You don't like what some of them do?
"Your friends are a bad influence",
said the boy who smokes weed daily
I know they're not perfect angels
but then again we're all human
You swear I'm just like them
I'm not going to lie,
In some ways I am
But in others I'm not
My friends are just that, my friends
I am not them, they're not me
So don't try to lump us all in one category

Beeper Messages   *April '00*

There's this little thing we do
when one's thinking about the other
We send little messages via pagers
Just to say "hello", or whatever
"Hi baby" was popular, and
we'd send "besos" back and forth-
You know, "kisses" in Spanish
And we'd type in "I miss you"
when one of us vanished
We had a few beeper wars,
but those were short-lived
And soon we relayed messages
like "I love you" spelled out,
Or in code, one-four-three
and then there were was the ever popular
"Lets go to bed",
You know...
for when we were feeling a little horny....

The Island of Paradise   *March '00*

What a strange place
I didn't ask to come here
I didn't try to get here
But I am here

I knew this place existed
because friends of mine have visited
Some even moved there
and they told me of its wonders

But I didn't figure I'd ever go
I'm not much of a traveler
besides from what I hear
It can be a very costly fare

But now that I am here
I see how right they are
This place is magnificent by far
and so full of splendor

This little island is paradise
and though it rains sometimes
It's important to realize
rain is healthy helping life flourish

But should tropical storms
and monsoons begin to plague
You should leave unless
You don't mind certain, and serious loss

New England and Then Wheaton   *April 8, '00*

Let's see,
It was me, my man,
His brother, and their friend
driving up to New England
To a party with drinking and smoking
(Oops my bad, he doesn't drink
It's against the Quran-
Apparently though Allah said it's cool
for Muslims to pass around the bong)
The party was good,
People, laughs, fun,
Yes! An open bar.
And Steve and I took a break
to have our private party in the car

The next day was a drive a little further north
to Wheaton College where they would perform-
The main reason for the trip
When we got there we cased the place
in between bouts of horseplay
We met with more of his friends,
and I lagged behind as greetings were made
'Cuz I didn't want to be in the way
to my surprise, and three times my pleasure,
My baby reached back to pull me up to his side
and introduced me as his "girl"
To his colleagues in the music world

A few hours later it was time
for sound checks and the show
My baby's group was the first to go
and not for nothing
but his group,
especially his brother and friend,
had a pretty good set
Damn, who would've thought they could actually rip shit
Back at the hotel, Steve and I relaxed in our room-
More specifically in the shower.
For about an hour
Before we joined his friends
Sitting around, snacking on food
talking about the show, music, and other things
until about four or five in the morning
when we finally retired to our room,
to fall asleep in each others arms
Knowing I'd get to do that a lot in the upcoming days
We were going to California together soon

California, Here We Come   *April 20, '00*
Ten days and nights in a row
California, a nice break
from New York and its cold April snow
Visiting my family, his friends
Enjoying some nice Cali weather
I'm so glad my baby and I are going together
We'll relax and play
under the California sun
But even if it rains
We're still gonna have fun
Because I'll be there with my man
Hell, the man of my dreams
with no curfews to keep
and no outside pressures
Just me and my baby
Just him and his lady

To...   *April '00*
To be in your arms
and press myself against your chest
Especially when it's bare
To hear your heart beat
To run my fingers through your hair
To look into your eyes
and introduce our souls
To kiss your lids when your eyes are closed
To kiss your back,
the tip of your nose
To nibble on your ear
To hold your hand
To hold you near
To touch your stomach
To feel your legs

To pinch your ass
To smell your scent
To see your face
and know what it's like to hug you
To kiss your lips
and know what it's like
To make love to you

Thank You Baby   *April 22, '00*
Thank you baby
for taking care of me
when I fell sick
with bronchitis
on the second day of our trip.
For buying my medicine
Making sure I took it
Making sure I stayed warm
And ate well too
I was surprised,
You stayed by my side
Even though you could have
Fallen ill too
Especially after all the hugs,
and kisses you showered me with
So thank you baby,
for being there
Your love is an incredible gift

California Fun   *April 24, '00*

Beaches and parks,
Seafood dinners
Just the two of us
Strolling along boardwalks
Making jokes,
Getting close,
Watching sunsets
and taking long drives
Talking about feelings,
insecurities and pain,
Comforting each other
until we're better again
Hugging each other,
Making love
under the moon,
Listening to the ocean
as we kiss,
California with my baby;
I'm loving it

Makin' Waves   *April 24, '00*
Sitting on the beach with my baby
under the afternoon sun
Watching the waves collapse
Amazed by its beauty
Along with the admirers
walking along the shoreline,
or leaping into the sea head-first
The waves, a vehicle for our leisure
The magnificent ocean crashing for all of us

Under the cover of night,
I sneak onto our patio
Peering through the trees
thoroughly amazed to see
that the ocean still breaks onto the shore,
slicing through the silence of the darkness.
There are no beach-goers to jump in,
No surfers, No sunbathers.
No children collecting water for sandcastles
As parents sit nearby
Yet, the ocean continues to make its splendid waves
It turns out the glorious display was not for us after all
The sea breaks onto the coast even when no one's there
It doesn't make waves for me or for you,
It just makes waves, just 'cuz that's what oceans do

Laguna Beach   *April 27, '00*
On his uncle's beach house patio
We have the house to ourselves
I sit on his lap, wrapped in a blanket
and lean back in his arms
We had just come from dinner
and also a fight
So here we were making up
talking all through the night
About Nicole and Sandra
and the rest of his lovers
and we talked about his concerns-
Like what's-his-face from Boston
among some others
We listened, and talked,
and talked, and cried
Under California's vast skies
with the ocean breaking on the shore nearby
After a few hours,
when there was more laughter than tears
we went indoors to make love,
and obliterate the rest of our fears

Silly   *April 27, '00*
Honestly, I think your worries are silly
Furthermore, I think they're unjust,
But I won't belittle them
because I know for some reason
Your pain is still real
so I take care, and comfort you
the best I can until you are relaxed
trying to understand how you feel
and at the same time
trying to figure out what the fuck is the big deal

Crocodile Tears   ***April 29, '00***

Countless times I held you in my arms
as you wept into my chest
It hurt me deeply to see you in pain
Feeling misunderstood,
Confessing insecurities, and confusion
and struggling with your demons
How I wished I could erase them from your life
or at least help you carry them
I knew how much you were hurting
and so, like the good woman I am,
I was there for you
in any way I could be
Anything to rid you of your anguish
Anything to make sure you were okay
Whether it's putting my needs behind yours
or simply wiping tears away,
Too bad I wouldn't find out for a long while
that they were the tears of the King Crocodile

In the Air   *April 30, '00*

Alarm sets in as I realize
the chance of us sitting together
is getting slim
As take-off time nears
I swear, my fears
have reached an all time high
Since not one person
empathizes with my plight
and agrees to switch seats on the flight
"Would you mind trading seats
so I could sit next to my wife?"
Now I know it was just a ploy
to be seated next to each other
But my heart fills with such joy
Nothing ever sounded so right
Me, being his wife
and for a moment I forget my paranoia
Living in complete euphoria...

Brought back to reality
by the voice of the stewardess
We continue our search until
a sweet woman agrees to our request
She gives up her chair
So he can hold me,
And during the flight
we talk about our trip,
how we're glad that we came
and at some point, I do something to him...
Until he does the same…

Places   *April '00*

In my Jeep.
In his bed.
Or in my friend's instead.
On a plane.
On the roof.
In the shower.
On his floor.
Against his friend's bathroom door.
Near the beach.
On a patio.
In my cousin's house.
In sinks.
On his parents couch.
On mine too.
In a hotel room with food.
In a kitchen.
At his brother's.
Out near the bay.
In the park after dark.
In a rented Ford.
In the middle of the day.
In a parking lot.
In a Pathfinder, with hot tea...
These are just some of the places...

Physical Therapist   *May 8, '00*

You lay face down on the bed
I console you with tender strokes
against your bare back
How beautiful it is
that I can put you at ease
with just a few loving touches
But as you listen to my words of love,
the blaring ring of your phone cuts me off
You answer, and sit up to chat
as I continue to lovingly caress your back.
Careful not to speak to me
you signal to show the stroking is good
and again to say that I should
continue with more of the same
Apparently, the conversation's too intense to interrupt
and my name's not important to share
When asked what you were doing at the moment
you don't even tell your little friend I'm there
Your body language-
Your entire demeanor changes
and within a minute or two,
I go from your girlfriend
to a physical therapist
Quietly tending to my injured client
Careful to stay in my place- the background
Doing only my duty of massage
so my patient can handle his affairs
I know it's female on the line,
A weird vibe takes over my soul
Someone you've been with before
It turned out to be Nicole

The Ex-Sex Hex   *May 9, '00*

I see you keep in touch with her
I see she's not the only one
Remember, when you went to Boston
and you visited Sandra
chilling in her house,
relaxing on her couch
while she and her roommate
played musical chairs with your lap?
So now let me get this straight-
It's okay for you to keep up with girls
with whom you've had sex
Or messed around with somehow
But you become apoplectic
if I talk or hang out with
one of my guy friends.
My gosh, you're so complex
But I think I figured you out
It scares you to think that I could be just like you
That my male friends are more than that;
People that I've seen in the nude
I know why you have trouble accepting
my camaraderie with men
It's because there has never been a female
with whom you've just been friends
Yes, maybe after you stop sleeping together
she remained in your life
and settled for the role of "companion"
since you refused to give her more
I know why *they* keep in touch
But tell me why do you?
It's not out of courtesy, so it must be
you want something from them
Maybe you like them sweating you,
knowing you could have them again
Or maybe you keep them around

So that you'll have a steady supply
In case your new well runs dry
Whatever the reason,
It's disrespectful to me
and it lets me know
I'm not as special as you say
Because if I was,
you'd make them all go away

His Ph.D. is in Hypocrisy   *May '00*
An alum of Boston University
where you majored in Psychology and Philosophy
Yea, your Bachelor's degree is in those subjects
But your Ph.D. is in hypocrisy
How else do you explain
why it's Ok for you
to have messed with two girls
when we first started out
yet my kiss in Boston still haunts you
Guys who are just my friends calling me
plagues your mind
But it's cool for you
to keep in touch with girls you know...
In the Biblical sense, of course
You lecture anyone who drinks
Yet chill with those who smoke weed
Preaching alcohol is wrong
According to the Quran
But if it bans drinking
I'm sure weed is out of the question
But apparently for that,
You've made a concession
See Jesus turned water into wine
Never did Mohammed turn roses into trees

But there you go having at least one blunt a day,
Please,
All the while preaching about Islam
Praising yourself because of your beard
And because you make most of your prayers
And fine, so you don't eat swine
Only animals with split hooves that chew the cud
But how funny is it
that afterwards you sit back and smoke bud
Granted alcohol is banned
But the Quran also does not condone
pre-marital sex or making money
rhyming on a microphone
after which you're gonna
again sit back and smoke marijuana
Double standards run your mind
But as long as you're the beneficiary
You don't seem care...
I just know your ass better not say another word
about me not covering my hair
or what I should and should not wear

The Competition   May '00

He mentions a girl's name in passing
I seethe with jealousy
Biting my tongue so I won't ask
if they had seen each other nude
My concern was not out of fear of being crude
but rather fear of hearing the answer
Surprised off my ass if it was "no",
Though I was more often disappointed
because, in the past my man had been such a ho
I began to hate females
that look like the type he might have done

And I drove myself crazy
one weekend I spent in Boston
Analyzing girl after girl
wondering if we had him in common
Or if we one day would
Leading me to hate all women
They were *all* my competition
I don't know why I feel this way,
or why his past is causing me such agony and pain
The only thing I do know
before I fell in love with him I was sane

Bad, Heathen, Christian Girl   *June '00*
Yes, we are from two different worlds
with different cultures and values,
languages and principals
I'm comfortable with who I am
I can still learn more about his background
and spend time with him
without abandoning my beliefs
It bothers me that the concept isn't mutual
He worries I'll make him forget who he is;
His family worries that too-
That I'm a negative influence over him,
Never mind that he's committed plenty sins
without my help
Never have I complained about his prayers
or have I told him to cut down his beard
even though many of our peers
consider a beard of his length weird
I never tried to encourage him
to go against his religion or his morals-
He does that all on his own
I'm not saying I'm not perfect,

Lord knows I'm no pearl
But how all of a sudden
did *I* become the bad, heathen, Christian girl?

Family Relations   *June '00*
His father looks at me
He still smiles
But because he feels he has to
It's no longer sincere
He's no longer happy I'm there

His mother smiles at me too
I can't tell if she means it anymore
But if she doesn't
she hides her contempt better
And still acts like she did
When I first met her

Things have changed between me
and his father and his mother
But at least they are still the same
Between me and his brother
We still get along
His smile is still real
I sense it when he talks
He's still sincere, and he likes me
Unlike the rest of the family

Turkey Wings   *June 15, '00*

I think I know why they don't like me
They think I'm a heathen
They don't think I'm good enough
for their precious Steven

Because I'm not Muslim
they think I'm the biggest sinner
And his father made a huge issue
over turkey wings my mother made for dinner

That's right- TURKEY WINGS
See, it wasn't halal meat;
Meat killed in the name of God
The only kind of meat Muslims can eat

There was no need to make such a fuss
So fine, he just won't eat the wings
But his father continued to complain
about that and so many other things

I'm not Muslim, or Arab
I don't cover myself from head to toe
I eat meat bought in the supermarket
And, yea, I'm probably a ho

I know Steve is taking it to heart
trying to be the perfect Muslim
But one thing his dad fails to notice
is I'm not trying to stop him

Why do you think I'm a bad influence?
I don't try to make him do anything
Well, unless it's for his own good
Like getting him to stop smoking

I have news for you though
No matter what is it you think I do
Your son does pretty much
whatever the fuck he wants to

I know how you feel about me
Not being of your religion, creed and race
But the really fucked up part
is that you have the nerve to still smile in my face

Muslim Melodrama   *June '00*
We're having a problem
Keeping our relationship intact
What the fuck is wrong?
Is it because I'm black?

I don't think that's it-
He says he likes my skin's dark hue
And he claims he likes my lips,
my hips and the kinks in my hair too

It must be our cultures since
we come from different worlds
Women must cover themselves in his
even the little girls

But I am from America
"Where the women are free"
to wear a sweat suit, a halter top
or a skirt above their knee

47

Even though I don't cover my hair
or make prayer five times a day
I'm still a God fearing person
who worships Him in her own way

I never tried to change my man
I think his lifestyle is fine
But I can appreciate his culture
without accepting it as mine

He shouldn't try to change me
or judge me just because
I have one or two faults...
just like *he* does

I know I am not perfect
There again, neither is he
But if my way is too much for him
then I guess we weren't meant to be

The Sole Owner of My Heart   *June '00*

You're my heart's sole owner
and the only owner of my soul,
The first to have either,
and yet you have both
They came to you as a set
Such power you have over them
I don't quite know what to expect
so please do be careful,
I want you to be in my heart
and next to my soul forever
That's how long
I want us to be together
To be friends, and lovers

To be your baby,
Yours for the taking
All the while forsaking
whatever men cross my path.
And not because of an obligation
that I have to you,
But because you're the man I want
and because nobody else will do
So here I am, all yours
Loving you, the love of my life,
With all my heart and soul
You're the man with whom
I want to grow old

Purpose   June '00
We all have purpose
He is to be my husband-
Father of my young

A Sexy Guy   June 23, '00
A sexy guy
With long hair,
Sharp features,
and matching wit
Beautiful eyes,
Matching body
A friend of a friend of a friend
Who, yes, wants to be my *friend*
He's interested in me
I give him the once over again
But there's a small problem
He's not my man

It'll Be Good For Him   *June 25, '00*

Why does my man have to leave
For a country halfway around the world?
Why does he have to call Lebanon home
For eight weeks of summer?
It'll be good for him, I know
A great chance to learn his language,
and meet relatives, no doubt
A great chance for me to catch up with old friends
and even take some ballet lessons
But why does he have to go so far away
and for such a long time?
I'm trying not to be selfish-
I know it'll be good for him,
But it's gonna be horrible for me
Imagine how lonely I'll be,
The whole summer without my baby
Not to mention, I'll be riddled with worry
with Lebanon in its state of political unrest
I don't want him to end up
With bullets or shrapnel in his chest
Nonetheless,
It's a great opportunity and
it'll be good for him, I know
So I'll give him my genuine blessing
with the gift of a care package for the plane
Telling myself over and over again
He's not leaving me,
He's going to do a good thing
Learning his culture and religion...
And again...it'll be good for him

Special   **June 28, '00**

You're very special to me
So special,
That you have the distinct honor
of being the first man I ever loved
Like I never loved another
My love for you is real,
I feel it every time I look at you,
hear your voice,
or think about you
Looking into your eyes,
is like touching your soul
Listening to you speak
is like a window into your heart
My dreams, both day and night
are of you
And I know our love is real
For after all this time,
the butterflies still come
I can't believe the incredible love
I found in you-
or how intense this thing called love is

When We Have Our Kids   *June '00*
We'll get married someday
and well have our kids
Two girls, two boys,
A boy and a girl-
It really doesn't matter to me
As long as we're one happy, healthy family,
And I know we will be;
Living somewhere off in Long Island
in the years to come
With our precious children
and with you,
The love of my life,
as my husband

It's the Way   *June '00*
It's the way we talk;
The way you call me several times a day
Just to say hi, or to see if I'm okay
It's the way you look at me,
It's your passionate kisses,
It's the way you caress my heart and soul,
It's the way you lose total control
When we make love to each other,
it's the way we protect one another
Both from harm, and from ourselves,
It's the way we became friends,
Confiding innermost thoughts and fears
It's the way you hold me when I'm scared,
The way you shield me from my pain,
The way you call out my name,
The way you drive me insane,
It's the way you steal my breath away,
It's how you love me every day

Your Ocean   *June 30, '00*

How sweet it is to hear your voice
So soothing and comforting,
Save for a few of your personal affects
you left behind in my care,
it's all I have right now
since an entire ocean separates us
And it will for two months
I miss you much
I know you miss me too
And I feel you should be aware
Though you're over there,
And me over here,
You have nothing to fear
'Cuz I'm your ocean,
Your own private sea
Making waves for you, and for us
Even though you're not right here next to me

Whatever It Takes...

Eight Weeks   *July 1, '00- August 14, '00*
It's only been a day since you left
But I miss you so much already
I can't wait for you to return to me
There are two whole months until then
But in the meanwhile,
we'll email and write
to keep over seven thousand miles

Ok, we're up to week two
A letter's in the mail for you
Is there one in the mail for me?
How are classes, your friends?
Did you get to meet your family?
Oh you're not checking email?
Ok, well that's fine
I'll just drop you a line
the old-fashioned way
I'm doing alright over here
though I miss you like crazy
Don't worry though,
I'm still your baby

Three weeks since you left
Two since I last heard from you
Missing you endlessly

Longing for your arms
Yearning for your lips
Hoping you're okay
Praying for you everyday
Forever mentioning your name
to anyone who will listen
Wishing I could talk to you more
I miss you so much
I miss holding you
I miss your touch
Guess I'll just have to wait patiently
for you to return
Then we could be together again
and maybe plan a trip to Virginia Beach
for the weekend
Hurry home sweetheart
so we can make up for lost time
I really love you baby,
I'm so glad you're mine

I sent letter after letter
The count is up to four so far
One for each week you've been away
I'm hearing from you less and less
but maybe my letter will come today
Before I forget, I did get your beep
saying you love me
It meant so much to me
That was really sweet
Though I miss you terribly, I am doing well
Seeing friends and family
Making a trip or two
Taking up new hobbies
All the while making waves for you

I sent you another letter,
One for week five
I gotta ask you-Are you still alive?
Well, I know you must be-
You sent my grandmother a postcard
but there's nothing ever in the mail for me
And here, the postman thinks I'm an idiot
For charging him every time he rings the bell
He only shakes his head and shrugs
Shit! You're putting me through hell
Why don't you write me
like you said you would?
Did you forget about me over there?
Funny, I didn't think you could

It's been one and a half months
You got a piece of mail
For each week of your program
and still I wait for yours in vain
With only a static-filled phone call
two weeks apart to sustain
me through this tough time
that you're away
Oh my gosh, at long last a letter
Open it quick!
What does it say?
You tell me of some friends
and some sights you've seen
family you met
and foods you've eaten
No real "how are you?"
No, "I miss you" either
Don't get me wrong
I'm glad that you're having fun
but if you cross out my name
That letter could've been for anyone

The last day of the program
and the start of week seven
I send you an email
Not expecting your reply,
but I get a response
the very next day
You miss me, you say
and you sign it with love
But I question your words
because your actions speak louder
And they're barely above a whisper

The seventh week has come and gone
and now the eight is here
You should be home in a few days
I'm happy, but I'm sad
I know something happened over there
It must have for your contact
with me to suffer so greatly,
until the program drew near
Only now that your newfound friends are gone,
Do I have some email from Lebanon
Oddly enough, you say you're skeptical of me
and of what I've been doing!
Aah...and here's a special treat,
Another phone call from the east
You ask if I forgot about you
Because heaven forbid,
I didn't return your email promptly
What are you crazy?
Baby I've been making waves for you all along
Were you making waves for me?

Anxiety Attack   *August 18, '00*

A nervous me approaches the door
that I've gone through so many times before
This time things are different
I can feel it in my heart
Something has happened
during the time we spent apart
Anxiety fills my soul
Questions fill my head
Will you be glad to see me?
Do you still love me?
Will you still think I'm pretty?

The door opens,
The most handsome man steps outside
Pulls me close, and hugs me tight
You kiss me full on the lips
but I know something's wrong
Deciding to ignore it for the time
Telling myself it was just my mind
Playing cruel tricks

You invite me in to show me things
From your trip
Present me with a necklace and some other gifts
including some for my family
You show me some drawings you sketched
When something catches my eye
Someone named Lana had doodled your name
With a big, red heart nearby
A flag of the same color goes up
But I push that aside too
Because we're going to be late
For our date
with my friends for the movies
And to be honest, I was just so happy to see you

We planned to spend the night out together
at the end of our evening
But things were not meant to be
So we go back to your home
to make love in your room
But as I lay here with you,
it feels like a lie
Things seem so different
it *has* been a long time
So maybe that's why-
But no, there's something in my heart
telling me there's something different about yours

In the morning, I feel strange and unhappy
Crying, I prepare to leave,
when you stop me,
You knew exactly what was wrong
and reassuring me of your love,
convince me to stay for breakfast
After which you show me pictures;
Guys and girls doing random things
A brief story behind them all
But one girl in particular strikes me as odd
Sociologically, her face
keeps appearing in the most random of places
I ask who she is, but I already figured
Nonchalantly, you reply "Oh, that's Lana"
Hmm, she's the one who drew the picture

What the word...?   *August 22, '00*

Outside my friend's house
prepping for family trip
to Virginia for a visit with my father-
A trip that *should've* included Steven
except that he hadn't bothered
to keep in touch for two whole weeks
until that day,
when he called with very little to say
Something was amiss
It had taken too long to hear from him
Something unheard of for us
and women's intuition is a wretched curse
So preparing for the worst,
Against my better judgment
I ask "Do you love me?"
"Of course I do".
"Fine," I say,
"But did you kiss anyone else while you were away?"
He didn't answer me,
He didn't have to
I'm fluent in *Stevenese*
That meant "Yes"
Still, I continued to press-
"Who's the girl?"
"You don't know her."
I wanted to strangle him
But once again,
With my woman's way of knowing,
I let him know I already knew who
"So did you sleep with her?"
"No" he answered straight out.
"Did she go down on you?
Tell me what happened?"
Silence was his answer,
Proving that it's not always golden

I asked one more time
Give him one more time to confess
"Did she go down on you?" I demanded
This time, the fool answered,
"Yes"

You're Mad?!   *August 22, '00*
You finally admitted you cheated
Naturally, I have a problem with it
but *you* are the one who starts the fight
You are the one who throws a fit
How can you be mad at me for getting upset?
How can you be mad at me for starting to fret?
Oh, wait, I see-
You think I'm upset
because I didn't use my opportunity to sleep around.
Well, that seems fair
A logical explanation
There's just one thing I don't get,
How the fuck are *you* the victim here?
I love you with all my heart
I waited faithfully for you to come back
passing several chances to cheat
even though I didn't have to
So why are you mad?
Because my heart, mind, body and soul
stayed true to you,
while yours strayed from my bed to hers?
and with no apparent reason-
You say she's not prettier, you don't love her,
You didn't stop loving me,
She's not better in bed than I am
And you weren't really all that horny
Did I neglect you?

Disrespect you?
Tell me, what did, or didn't I do?
I can't believe the shit that just went down
That you could do something so mean,
so hurtful, so bad
Then try to pity yourself
by flipping the whole thing on me
You have no fucking right to be mad

Crazy   **September 1, '00**
I know I'm crazy to take this trip with him
And take this shit from him
But I'm not ready to give up this fight
If there's a chance we can make it
I want to try,
As long as he's willing to do the same
Maybe this trip
will grant us some much needed time together
to reconnect and reconvene
Some rough times lay ahead I know
There's a lot for us to overcome
But it's worth it to me to try for us
because the other half of us is you
and I love you and still want to be with you
So bad in fact,
that I'm swallowing my pride,
and going against better judgment and advice
inviting you along to Boston
for this, our final test

You Don't Talk To Me Anymore   *September 3, '00*

You barely spoke to me on the way up
You're barely speaking to me now
So unconcerned with my feelings
Too wrapped up in your self-righteous convictions
Guilty pleasures, and pretend pity party
to take time to talk to me
You're not too busy however
to try to entice me in sexual acts
Settling for a do-it-yourself technique
rubbing up against me in my sleep,
until you come on my back
You didn't spend many waking hours with me
though you said that you would
Of course,
You also told me you wouldn't mess with another girl
Apparently you're not good at keeping your word
But you're really good at speaking cross ones
And you've gotten real good at disrespecting me
Lying about your whereabouts
When you were chilling with some chick,
Using my cell phone to answer the beep
of some other girl you slept with

All I wanted was to spend time with you,
and talk things out so we can move on together
Instead, you're insistent on being mean
and attacking me for trivial things
Getting mad because you don't think I defend you
should my friends talk bad about you
Little do you know I do stand up for you,
Little do you know all that I do for you
But you don't seem to notice
or at the very best, you just don't care

63

You're determined to make mountains out of molehills
Like me talking to my friends about our situation
Who the fuck else am I supposed to talk to
With you not giving two fucks about us
Not wanting to hear anything I have to say
Unlike you, my friends want to make sure I'm Ok
So yes, arms will hug me, and go around my shoulder
You don't have to get mad at that
Or because I sat on my friend's lap
Because all he was trying to do was dry the tears
that you wouldn't

Bad Dream   *September 3, '00*

It's four in the morning
I'm having a nightmare
I wake up in a panic
You're next to me,
but you're not there

Laying Without You *September 3, '00*

Laying beside you.
At the same time without you
Holding my pillow
where you used to be
Feeling my tears,
instead of your heartbeat
My loneliness caressing me,
My pain, and my fears,
watching over me,
And my pillow-
My only means of support
Even though you're laying right next to me-
in the same bed-
So close that I can hear you breathe-
There's distance between us
So much so that
you're not even really there
Can't help but wonder if you ever were
So forgive me for crying
because it's hard
to lay here helplessly
next to the corpse that was our love

You Said You Loved Me, But You Lied

I Try Not to Call You   *September 7, '00*

I try not to call
but I find I always do
Now how is it that
I'm the one still sweating you
You did wrong to me
after I gave you all my love
You said you felt the same way
and you swore to heaven above
that there was no one else
No one could take my place
but apparently all it took
Was red hair and some matching lace
Now I must find the strength
to leave "us" behind
It's the only way I can keep
from losing what's left of my mind

Your Death   *September 9, '00*

Your love meant so much to me,
But tragically, you died during your travels
Now the whole day long,
But especially at night
I think about us
And the future we would've-
Could've had.
Those dreams are gone now,
They died when you did
Strangely enough, your death wasn't physical
Your body is still around
It's your soul that resides six feet under ground
You're such a different person
Since you came back from your trip abroad
Or rather from the broad on your trip
And now, now all I have are memories
of time we spent,
Trips we took,
Snapshots of us in my picture book,
conversations we had,
games we played
secrets we shared...
and the love I thought we had made

You Used to Say You Love Me   *September 9, '00*

You used to say you love me-
And I believed you
The funny thing is
you believed yourself too
Unfortunately, it turned out
your love wasn't real
But you're the lucky one
The beneficiary of love and affection
Unlike me, who suffers from pain, and rejection
Shit, you got off easy-
In more ways than one I might add
By means of a certain skanky chick.
Running fingers through her hair
While she slobbered all over your dick
occurring more than one instance
over a five week span
Something that shouldn't have come to pass
if you were really my man-
If you were really thinking about me-
If your love for me was sincere-
If you really did care-
You would have told me on your own
instead of me having to interrogate you over the phone
after which you had the nerve to get upset
that I was hurt
condemning me right and left
claiming the main reason for my pain
was because I didn't mess with other guys
Getting even more pissed off with my
who, what, where, when and whys
I don't know what to say to you
For fear of how you'd react
In fact,
I don't know much of anything
At one time I knew you loved me

That was one thing of which I was sure
But now after all this...
I just don't know anything anymore

You Told Me You Loved Me   ***September 16, '00***
You told me you loved me
You were so cold about it
But even though I doubted it
it was a comfort to hear those words
come from your lips
They certainly didn't come from your heart
Silly me, even knowing that
I still wanted to be with you
because I loved you that much
And for a minute I thought
you loved and wanted to be with me too
In actuality you did
but you wanted everything your way
Who knew being with you
had such a high price to pay
Pride, dignity, self-worth, my convictions
I'd probably end up even having to switch religions
Sacrificing all I believed in
Just to be with an ass named Steven?
I'd have to forfeit everything
What kind of love is that?
Not the true kind,
I know that much
You told me you loved me
It's you just talking out of your neck
I gotta admit though, I'm curious to hear
What would roll out of your mouth next

You Told Me You Loved Me Again September 19, '00

You told me you loved me again
and that you cared about me
This time I didn't believe you
You already proved many times over
You didn't have my back
You hurt me and lied to me
Disrespected me and much more
Used me, abused me,
Cheated with a seventeen year old whore,
And after she was said and done
You had the audacity to say that I'm the only one-
Words just falling out of your mouth again
You don't even know the meaning of what you said
I don't know, maybe it was a feeble attempt
to get me back into bed
It may have worked a few days ago
But things are starting to change
I'm stronger now, and less confused,
Unwilling to participate in your cruel games
Because of this strange phenomenon called love
I wanted to work this out
Try to restore our relationship
Salvage what's left of our friendship
But it's too late for all that now
You already showed me the man you've become...
And I can't love *him*

Yet
September 26, '00

How is it you stopped doing the things you used to
Yet the things you tell me stay the same?
How can you claim your love for me so intense
yet be intimate with a woman by another name?
How do you say those three words with such conviction
yet have no problem being with other women?
How do you push your love inside other girls
yet get upset should I chill with a guy friend?
The answer my darling is you don't love me
yet you insist that you do
So ok, you're not at fault for your lack of feelings for me
yet lying and cheating, I still blame you

Grievin'
September 30, '00

Alone in my room grievin'
Cuz you had me believin'
for the longest time
I was the one you wanted
But you were just conceivin'
A scheme so deceivin'
You planned on bereavin'
me of my happiness
to make yourself feel good
and stroke your own ego
So here I sit,
Because of you Steven
My emotions seethin'
My chest heavin'
Having trouble breathin'
Without any reprievin'
And I can't take it anymore
I won't take it even
So with a heavy heart,
I must say, I'm leavin'

71

The Saddest Love Letter   *October 2, '00*

Poured my out soul in a letter to you
About my feelings, and Lana,
the way you treated me
and how I'm gonna
have to finally call it quits
because I'm getting nothing but hurt
since recently you've taken to
treating me like dirt
I hope we can still be friends
but after everything ends
I don't think that's too likely
because if you were my friend from the start
You would never have crushed me
You still claim to love me,
Which is real hard for me to believe
Especially with you trying to flip this on me;
You know- that I want to move on to some fictitious guy
Questioning my love for you
When it was *yours* that was a lie
Doubting *my* feelings, actions, virtues, and intent.
But what you fail to see,
This is all about you and your ego and it always has been
You told me before
Things weren't too different
between you and your other women,
Save, you didn't love them
the way you allegedly loved me
Now, you want to hear something funny?
Or maybe fucked up is a better phrase
I write all this exactly one year
after our first date
expecting at least to hear
one last time from you
But your only response to my heartfelt letter
is a beep with the message "I love you too"

Every Day I Try

I Was...   *October '00*

I was your sweetheart
I was your partner
I was your lady
I was your baby

I was your confidant
I was your supporter
I was your girlfriend
I was your best friend

I was your lover
I was your fantasy
I was yours
Now tell me, what did that mean to you

Split Personality   *October '00*

Since we broke up,
I haven't been myself
Crying day and night,
Doing stupid things
Making little sense
And silly decisions
Not knowing where my head is
Or what to do next

73

I try to be strong
I try my hardest
My futile attempts
lead me to do stupid things
To myself, and to others

I'm on a constant quest to seek help
and protection from myself
To no avail, of course
My mind,
On a path of destruction
My body not far behind
Spinning out of control
at the same time,
trying to take control
to keep from falling
deeper and faster into this abyss
You helped create for me

Reality Kicks Ass   ***October '00***
In my elusive quest to be alright
I keep having to endure the same damned fight
I make believe you're still away
Since it seems like that anyway
I tell myself that you died,
Because in a sense you did
But lying to myself,
It doesn't' work too well
Because four minutes later
Reality comes back,
And that shit hurts like hell
It knocks me to the floor
and proceeds to kick my ass
Throwing out punches

With uncanny precision and accuracy
Before finally ending the bout
by spitting on me
That happens all the time,
Especially when I'm not lookin'
Reality sneaks up on me
…Commence the ass whoopin'

Dreams   *October '00*
Another day has passed
without talking to you
I should be another day stronger
But I'm not
And now it's time to let the night pass by
and turn into day
I thought I'd welcome the oblivion sleep offers
but no, sleep is my adversary
I don't rest much at night anymore
My mind racing 'til way past dawn
with images and questions of you and me,
And yes, of you and her
When sleep finally does grace me
it comes as a mixed blessing
My anxieties transforming into vivid nightmares
Ritually plaguing me several times in just one night
Confused, and dazed
I wake up to a nervous and anxious me
glad to realize it was just a dream, I relax

In those dreams where my life isn't threatened
They are of you and I
Laughing, kissing, hugging, talking
or one comforting the other
Essentially, everything we're not doing now

And in my dreams, we're going to make it
because in my dreams our love is great
Unconquerable even
Confused, and dazed
I wake up to a relaxed and joyful me,
Angry to realize, it was just a dream, I get anxious

Sometimes my dreams mirror real life
Where you and I are not together
and you're with someone else instead
Confused, and dazed
I wake up to a crying me,
The tears already streaming down my face
Realizing my dream is reality
The tears just fall harder and faster

The Exchange   *November '00*
I have several things of yours that you want back
And though I'm tempted to rip them to pieces
I'll return them intact
as long as you do the same
with some items of mine

I've postponed seeing you for as long as I can
but I think it's finally time
to see each other
and get this exchange over with
So I can get on with my life
and can get rid of your shit

But like I said,
I want my stuff back too
That includes my compact discs,
My books, my clothes,
and especially those pics of my tits!

You Are Not a Woman *November '00*

You are not a woman
Not in any way
And I don't just mean
'Cuz at the time
you were only seventeen
You disrespected another female
But you hurt yourself even more
You may think you're special
because my man accepted you into his bed
even though I was in his life
You may think you have something over me now
but tell me, are you any closer to being his wife?
You love him you wrote
But do you think he loves you?
And before you answer that
Did he tell you that he did?
And if so, do you think it's true?
He told me he loved me
Hell, he told me that, even after you
But I had the sense to stop believing him
So let me ask you this girlfriend
How special do you feel?
How often do you talk to him?
Do you think what you had was real?
And how did he treat you?
You followed him around like a well-trained puppy
And he complained about you
Calling you immature
while at night you gave him head
And parts of your body too
But do you think he cherished it
Do you think he cherishes you?
Did he make you his girl?
Or were you too just his fool?
Don't think you were better

We all know you're not
You're not worth half of me, little girl
But what do you know,
You're still dumb-I mean *young*
But hopefully you've learned from this
during the time you wallowed
that what goes around comes around and
No female, regardless of age
Who can do that to another
is worth the sperm she swallowed

If He Died   *November '00*

I don't know how to love him
At least not anymore
I don't know who he is
And I don't know how to care for him
At least not with my heart
I can't say I know this man
Though at one time I thought I did
I'm only familiar with his exterior now
The soul I once knew is no longer there
He talks to me harshly,
He touches me coldly,
Dismisses me swiftly,
Pushes me away boldly
If he were to pass on
I don't think I'd be blessed
with the tears to cry
Because the man I once knew,
The man I still love,
Unfortunately has already died
Leaving nothing but a selfish, cold, thoughtless
stranger inside

I Had Once Hoped   *November '00*

I had once hoped to be your wife
But with the recent spate of disrespect
I had to make a drastic change
and rid you from my life
Granted it wasn't easy
and I've been second-guessing
my decision since I made it
Though everything is still fresh
and hurts beyond belief
I can't let it get the best of me
I can't sit around and mope forever
That wouldn't be fair to myself
I can't go back with you either
That would be bad for my mental health
It's not that I expect you to try to return
But I couldn't take you back even if you did
'Cuz see, I refuse to be anyone's dummy
Hurt me once, shame on you
Hurt me twice, shame on me
I have to take care of myself
Put myself first
You sure as hell ain't gonna do it
In fact, you wanna know
The only thing you've done for me lately...
Shit.

Moving On   *November, ' 00*
We've been broken up for awhile
We've spoken only about thrice
And very few of the words
you've spoken to me have been nice
I'm trying to get over you
and continue on with my life
I can't believe the things that happened,
or that you gave us up for
A couple of dick-sucking nights with
Lana the Dingy, Red-Headed Whore
Still that's in the past, as are we
I have to move on so I do
I go out with my friends,
and I have a good time too,
But why in the hell is it
That I'm still making waves for you?

Hard to Swallow   *December '00*
What's hard to swallow, pun intended
is the fact you were gone for only two weeks
when your meat started rubbing
the inside of Lana's cheeks
Now how is that love for me?
How does that make me number one?
How can you be with me after her?
Where'd you get the nerve to call me hon?
I was a good thing you know,
But now you and I are through
You had your chance with me
And you blew it when she blew you

I Stroked Your Ego   *December, '00*

I stroked your ego,
Among other things
I nourished your soul,
and replenished your self-esteem
I nurtured your heart
and nursed your hurt
Never neglecting you
or pushing you aside
Always having your back,
Swallowing my pride,
Holding you when you cried,
Putting your needs right there beside mine
Because I loved you with all my heart
And for some strange reason,
after all you put me through
believe it or not, I still do

Newsflash   December '00

An Arab terrorist is victimizing women
Attacking all races, and religions the same
Ages ranging from seventeen to thirty
Though those twelve to sixty are fair game
Countless women have fallen prey
to the five foot ten felon,
Weighing in at 180 pounds
A beard an inch or two in length,
Hair color, a dark brown
His eyes are blue, his smile is charming
His voice is a deep bass
Other attributes, an attractive physique
And a very, very handsome face
But on the inside, he is horribly disfigured
covered with unsightly sores and lesions
He spews forth hypocrisy, twisted logic
and false words telling of false feelings
Once caught he will be charged with
Heartbreaking and entering,
Reckless abandonment,
Aggravated emotional assault
And making the victims feel
the whole episode was mainly her fault
Driven primarily by sexual greed
he is an extreme threat to women with hearts
so until he is captured, you ladies better take heed

Quick fix   *December '00*

It seems another woman
Has caught my man's eye
And her feminine wiles
Made me tell him good-bye

How could he share himself
with another lover
Was I not doing my part
Pleasing him under the covers?

Should I do the same,
Run to the arms of another
And hop into bed
With some random brother

It'd be a quick fix, but
After all's said and done
It won't be him I'd hurt,
But myself in the long run

The best thing to do
Is take a break from men
And get my head together
Before trying relationships again

Numbers   *December '00*

6 years before our first date
10 canceled ones after that,
111 days I've spent time with you since
22 nights as well
3 of them in a hotel
7 movies we saw in the theater
3 shows I witnessed you perform
2 visits to Ernesto's Italian restaurant
5 separate excursions to the beach front
3 times dining at Garden of Fantasy
4 to the Japanese place a few doors down
2 amusement parks
6 visits to your brother's apartment uptown
58 times we made love at least
20 women, or more you made love to
4 guys I knew before you
4 road trips to the New England area
5 trips in total
14 beautiful roses
25 other flowers
2 times we spoke, at least every day until the
2 months you were away
4 phone calls in that time
5 letters I mailed overseas
1 sent with you on the plane
1 letter sent to me from you
6 weeks it took for you to do
2 weeks away before you cheat
6 more until you told me
6 weeks more until I said goodbye, 'cuz for
52 weeks I lived your lie
12 months for your heart to freeze
365 days for things to turn
180 degrees

After You, Over You

Why, Again?   ***December '00***
Why did I go out with you?
Again, I mean-
Not in the first place
I guess I just longed
to see your face,
And to feel your embrace
after all this time
And had hoped that you seeing me again
would change your mind

Truth be told I've missed you
and I hoped the day you'd realize you missed me too

Alas, instead the evening starts out
with a summons for being in a park after dark
and so we'd both have to report to court
in about one month's time
But even though the outing
didn't really start out good,
I still wanted to hang out with the man
and try to work whatever magic I could

We ended up at a pool hall
where we played a few games
And talked about random stuff
that's when I realized it was definitely the end of us

85

Court   *January 19, 2001*

A few phone calls here and there
About the nineteenth day of the new year-
The day we'd have to appear
in court, and hopefully have our names cleared
Judgment day arrives
on a cold and rainy morning
and Steve and his father give me a ride
The latter complaining the entire way
but I ignore him because his son
is the reason
that we're here in the beginning
We pull up to the court building
and after finding our way in,
Steve apologizes for his father's behavior
but I could care less about that wretched old man
and whatever the fuck he has to say
I'm not concerned with that fool anyway

Steve's not much better because he says he has to leave
For prayer with his father,
And he does just that
Leaving me alone with a legal system
That screwed me by making me come back
on the second day of March
As things couldn't be much more harsh,
in disbelief that Steve got me in this mess
And that he's not supporting me
in this court mini crisis
I was faced with another dilemma-
I had no ride home,
And though the rain had let up
I was experiencing an internal downpour
Thankfully my best friend was around
And she drove all the way across town
to pick me up and console me

As I sat there bawling
I had to ask myself
When will my tears finally stop falling?

Court Aftermath   *February '01*
I'm alright, I think
At least I will be
I'm really appalled
that he still hasn't called
Nearly a month later
to see how things went for me,
Though I guess there was no real need
Since I know he was there
to witness my fate,
I saw him slip back into the room
moments before I was to stand before the judge
not bothering to acknowledge me,
or wish me luck
Still I was curious to hear what fate befell him
and was purely dumbfounded when
he tells me he was dismissed,
The motherfucka's free!
Shit! That's the second time he's gotten off without me!
It was so unfair
But what the fuck did he care
As long as his holier than thou ass
Got out of there.

I'm Alright, I Think   *March '01*

I'm alright, I think
Breaking up was hard
But somehow, someway
I'm fighting this
Somehow, someway
I'm making it through
Shit, I have to
I can't put my life on hold
Mourning the loss of my love,
Thinking of him
Or what once was,
So I do things to keep my mind clear,
Like hang out with my friends
Old and new ones,
Visit some cousins,
Movies by the dozens,
Tons of dates,
Some of whom are admittedly mistakes
But nonetheless,
At least now I'm in control
Of my situation and my destination
I'm doing me with no apology
With my new tough exterior
Shielding my inner turmoil from the world
All anyone sees
Is a pseudo-confident girl
In charge of breaking other people's hearts
At least the hurt won't be experienced on my part
No, not this time
I'm happy and in control of both my heart and mind
They're finally in sync
Yea I'm finally gonna be alright...I think

S(t)even Year Itch   *May, '01*

From start to finish
We lasted just a year
Things officially over
on the anniversary of our first date
Albeit,
The way it ended
I'm not filled with hate
things were not in vain
Because there was so much
packed into such a short time
From how we met
to how I left
Such power, such love,
Such pleasure, such pain
There were things that were so right
but those are things I'd never do again
Because the sun has set on our time together
By my own choice I walked away
Truth be told, though painful now
It would have been even more so to stay
I know I'll be alright,
I have no choice but to be
I just wish things could've turned out differently
That we could've ended up together
Creating new memories instead of reliving old ones
of late night talks,
Moonlit walks,
Our pet names,
Our beeper games,
Some really bad fights,
Leading to sleepless nights,
Beautiful flowers,
Making love for hours,
Posing for photos,
Going to his shows,

Dinner at our favorite restaurant,
Sitting out on the waterfront
My love for him
His alleged love for me
Refuted of course,
by his infidelity
So the sun has set on our time
And I'm slowly coming to terms with it
Soul searching,
Reading books,
Going out with friends
And just when I know I'm gonna be alright
I hear from you again,
Asking me to hang out...
And like a fool
I give in

Happy Hangin' Out   *June 3, '01*

You call me again and we hang out
A few days before my birthday
We hang out at the park by the water,
We take a walk,
We sit and talk
You take my hand
Just like you used to do-
the exact reaction I was looking for
At our last rendezvous

We go back to your place,
We chill, we eat,
Listen to some music, dance,
And when you see a chance,
You try to kiss me
I let you for a moment
But don't think I'm kissing you back
It just doesn't work like that
At least not anymore
I can't say that I trust you
To start this again
Though I had long hoped to make amends,
and start anew with you
But I'm through
My guards are up
And it's a good thing
Because a few days later,
I'm driving home in my car,
And my cell phone starts to ring...

The Phone Call   *June 6, 2001*

It's you...
Asking to talk,
About yourself, as usual
Apparently you're the sun
And the world revolves around you-
And your problems,
But I agree to talk
and help you out-
Like I used to
Listening to you spew
all his crap about love
(Something, as your former lover and friend,
I still don't think you understand)
and you go on and on
about how you feel like something's wrong-
Like you're broken
after witnessing disparities
Between your brother's relations with his girl,
And all the girls that have been a part of your world
So I suggest,
"Maybe you haven't found the woman you love yet,"
"Yea, maybe that's it,"
It killed me to hear you agree
Though if it's true, it explains a lot-
But now with my ego shot
With my last shred of hope gone
I know now I really, really have to move on...

Now   *August 2, 2001*

Now, things aren't the same
Not you, or my feelings
And plus I know what you're capable of
So, no my love
There's no more you and me,
and there's never going to be
I have long since moved on,
I've learned to live without you
and even how to be happy
There's no need to cry myself to sleep
for I'm used to being without you now
I've learned to manage somehow
Who would have thought
That I would actually be alright
without your presence in my life

I see your car every now and then
and even ran into you when
I was headed to meet up with my girl
Impressed not by you,
But the fact that we live in such a small world-
We chatted a few times when you called
inviting me to a dinner
Which I didn't care too much for-
Save to savor when you tried to kiss me
As you stood by my car door
Shifting your eyes down in embarrassment
After I pulled away from your lips
"That's alright I'm sexy," I said, "You couldn't help it"

Now I'm sure I have your numbers somewhere
But I don't care to dig them up
So if for whatever reason,
I need to talk to you,
I'll wait for you to call,

And you will, because you do
I'll probably see you again,
Maybe with or without plans
But on my part there's no effort or reason
For me to keep in touch with you, Steven
I got my life back
I found my mind too
In fact, I got a new man
And I just started graduate school
So you know what-
Believe it or not,
I'm cool

September 11, 2001
9:12 am Tuesday.
A wake-up call...
From...one of my best friends...
Something about...

two planes...crasHING...
THE TOWERS
NO!
My sister is down there
No this cant' be-
On comes the TV,
footage of the burning towers
and in less than two hours
both buildings collapsed
I got lucky.
My best-friend-sister-girl
made it out alive
But two thousand seven hundred forty-nine didn't
survive,
Not including two-hundred forty-four casualties from
other states,
the other two hijacked planes,
Or the twenty-four still unaccounted for

Muslims attacking America,
in the name of Allah
Islamic extremists using religion as a means to their end
Making threats to attack us again
Leaving Americans scared
and seething with rage
at the people who pray to the east,
not knowing the literal root of Islam...Peace

I no longer have affection for Steve or his family,
But thankfully, I had already been exposed
And I had once loved and learned from them
So I didn't believe
the lies being told
and propaganda set forth
about Muslims and the Arab world
freeing me of certain misplaced hate
for an entire people and their state
Not having a heart full of distrust and disdain,
Knowing Islam is not the root
of the evil than men do
But rather a scapegoat for a few
with unjust judgments and ill-intents
who shall be dealt with when God calls them home
So no need for vindictive plots seeking revenge
toward innocent Arab brethren
Living among us as doctors, teachers, neighbors, friends,
With shoulders laden with unjust blame
Because they pray to God using another name
And in this time of international crisis
amidst the aftermath
of a most horrific terrorist attack
I can wish them comfort
I can wish them peace
It seems I did learn a lot from Steven.
his purpose in my life is now finally rendered complete